POETIC ANARCHY
VOLUME 3

Bunny Wilde
Nate Colton
Mindy Semingsen
Tim Johnston
Thomas Kropp
Hannah Fletcher
Garrett Carroll
O. Marie
Matt Wall

Poetic Anarchy
Volume 3

w/ poems by

Bunny Wilde
Nate Colton
Mindy Semingsen
Tim Johnston
Thomas Kropp
Hannah Fletcher
Garrett Carroll
O. Marie
Matt Wall

Edited by Matt Wall

these poems were written during the week long
Poetic Anarchy workshop
held in the summer of 2022

for more information
please visit
www.poeticanarchy.com or
www.ihatemattwall.com/bloodshedpress

TABLE OF CONTENTS

Bunny Wilde

footsteps on the gravel...

flutter in my chest at 2 AM
when I'm raising the dead
weight of my pen
and an amused whistling
tickles my ear drums
like spiders dancing
on guitar strings
and if I'd just look out my window
I'd expect to see the moon face of death
singing with beams spreading his lips
calling me into that last light
and I'll whistle with him when I go
happy to take a late night stroll
because he's always promised to be there
in the end when I have nothing else
I cried for him before I slept
to wake to words I wrote for you to forget
and he came with a song for me

last night...

the fire consumed angels
and they were happy
to never shed
another tear for us
they cried their own names
and were thankful
for our bodies in the ditches
and the blood of the holy
running in the rivers
they loved the way we die
because we are fallen
and we have more light
so when their ashes settle
I'm gonna fill my cup
and drink to outer darkness

I wait for rain...

to speak
and I say please
wash the last part of me
from the thunderheads
hulking warships
cannons with the faces of clouds
to water the backs
of tigers in the grass
and ragged drunks
with spittle lips and old eyes
jerking their hips
away from the train station
down the street
and engines barking omens
below my half lidded window
the sky is hanging
like a dead mourning dove
from a dog's tongue
and I hear no rainspeak
to answer me in bullets for my relief
it will not come to make me clean
and the only part I have left
in the world tonight
is waiting

slip down...

under the scars
fat purple worms
spotted with suture marks
into the pulse of hope
with the flow and warmth
of your blood under those cords
that pulled you together
when lies forced razors
to scream red on the tiles
of the bathroom floor
you've let the worms go white
faded into ghost tracks
across your wrist
and beneath them the truth
you chose to live

Inside

you're playing
a falling game
heat coloring your lips
they go blue
like you lost all life
drowning in the screen
I'm a little sick
I like it
and you say
you bitch
you held me
you killed me
I say
I know
before you blow me a kiss

Outside

I wanted to bring you home
make you mine
peel you open
roll you on my tongue
swallow what's under that skin
but the swarm had come
whispering death
down onto your yellow fingers
so I walk on by
as the flies take you
you can rot for someone else

I woke up one Sunday...

and I had a new mouth
the mirror showed me
it was hanging on the left
and when I cracked my jaw wide
the opening between my lips
gave me the face of something
that might gnaw your soul out
my reflection was not something
I'd ever seen of myself before
my husband called his mother
she was a nurse
and while he barked into the phone
I swear I could see my eye and brow
slowly drooping down
until they were not mine
I watched the right side of my face
go paralyzed and slack
sagging like an old tit
and what I see now looks like a lie
being told to my face

                    I never learned...

how to wear my face
ugly with an obscenely big nose
it hurts
it's always hurt
people have hated it
hated me
because of this fucking face
and now that half of it hangs
paralyzed
everything the mirror always said
is more true than it's ever been
I'm afraid
I will never have my reflection back
I've been down on myself
for all my life
stomach torn over what I see
agonizing over my appearance
I could barely show myself
beyond my door
because I was so ashamed
of how I look
and I could rarely shower
without sobbing
could never fuck
without thinking
about how disgusting
I must be
and when I would want to cum
I would feel sick
because I knew
I look like a gorilla
the face I couldn't change
has changed itself
into something
that makes my heart break

and my tears burn
in my drooping eye
because I don't know
if I can do this
I don't know if I can learn
to love what was a mess
I'm howling
crying
tearing at my skin
I don't want this
I'm more than ugly
just let me be ugly again

Nate Colton

09/10/2019

The happiest day of my life
was on an October the 9th
I jumped out of bed
and re-shaved my head
showered, dressed
all looking my best
I made my way into town

The bus was on time
Early autumn sunshine
In brown beige tweed
my nerves wouldn't cede
I follow my feet
and where do they lead?

Straight into my friend Joe.

He wasn't initially invited
but I got drunk and scared he'd feel slighted
no card or note
Joe, the top bloke
Remembered the date
and not to be late, we bus together in haste.

The ride ends at the gates
to Wollaton Hall
a royal estate and Wayne Manor
atop a huge grassy hill
My nerves plague me still
walking my knees start to tremor

Yet...

His effect on me was so calming
It was just what I needed as

My nerves finally ceded
While walking the grounds
As we come around
Me and Joe
Face to face with a doe
I joked we should go
My day had been made

But this was just the beginning

Because...
The happiest day of my life
was on October the 9th
The day I married my wife

One Fall

A crowd of strangers
Fields of fingers
Face shines to heat seekers
Snapmares and arm wringers
Ranas and head scissors
Back drop full stop
Near fall, Big OOOOHHH!!!
Drop kicks and V triggers
Crowd down to a simmer
Taste of defeat is bitter
But losers can beat winners!

Epilogue

They have taken my grave!
I have no end
How can I die when I've nowhere to go?
When my brother won't budge up.

she asked

She's pretty much deaf
Likes to wear strange dresses in the cold
But she asks if I have children?
I'm glad I don't,
Yet.

Mondays Child

No wonder I hate Mondays
It reminds me that my mother was my hat
As I fell feet first from womb to tomb.
I am down to lose my eyes.

smiles up top

The Red 43 bus from City Centre to Bakersfield
Red line like those in my eyes
Pulsing nerves to whatever cortex in my brain
Identifies your image as I pull up up above you
Before the windmill, just passed the massage
parlour
Our eyes meet both behind glass
You smile before looking forward to board
I know you'll join me upstairs
Take the seat in front of mine
I sit up a little straighter conscious of my slouch
Belly like a bag of soft goods gets pulled back in
effort
You playfully pull a strand of your curly hair
straight
Smell like flowers I once walked past in Colwick
Wood
Your left hand is free
Mine is now too
I use it to press the bell for my stop
Determined to return the smile back up to you
The sun's too bright
Sheltering from the light
I lose sight of you.
Maybe next time.

                    burst of Venus

When the sea had calmed
From bubbling in blood and
The clam recoiled to the waves
The Sun bright behind clouds
And
Venus alone on the shore

dog like

Contorted around leather
breathing in an odd rhythm
Dreaming in thunder
of ending his father
What possessed the back to bow
in such an arched fashion

Seductive Juno turns his eyes
in on themselves
And they bare witness
to a sleeping Dog named
Zeus

Loe

It's not been going great
She can't hear to good
They whisper when she leaves her seat
Laugh loudly when she exits the room
A couple of us like the way she changes the
temperature
Greys differently to the others
Strides in shorts and solid steel and
Says "See you tomorrow" like one hand on a
sheathed sword

Mindy Semingsen

True Beauty

The happiest day of my life was
in the middle of an open field
many miles from anywhere

Laying on my back
the feel of dry grass
scratching my neck

The cool fall air
gives goosebumps
at this late hour

For the first time
witnessing the beauty
of the Wyoming night sky

Surrounded by new friends
sharing the magnificence
of a million stars
brighter than anything

Is this real?

It is otherworldly
hours pass
the awe does not lessen

Psychopath in Training

After what you've done
you look me straight
in the eyes
and smile
as I cling to my mother

I'm just another step
in your training

When I Learned to Appreciate the Average

Kneeling in the back
of a dirty supply closet
losing my mind
as my world fell apart

It was supposed to be
just another Thursday

What to Say

Do you plan on having kids?
No! Why not?

I don't know what to say
Why is it so hard
to talk to humans

I Am Not Okay

Standing room only
all packed in
no room to move

Loud cheering is
my whole existence
I cannot breathe

My Personal Hell

My personal hell
is a house party
I don't know anyone
small talk forever

I Am A Monster

I feel like a monster
feeding off the
suffering of others
as I sit in this
support group
healing over shared pain

Best Cure for a Panic Attack

Never underestimate
the healing power
of a cat on you shoulder
one on the legs
purring contentedly

You Broke Through

I never thought I would
truly trust a man
other than my father

You were so patient
you broke through
every wall

Hippo Squeaky Toy

Bright pink hippo
toy for my cats

Prominent position
on the cat tree

Happy face, yet menacing
Those big beady eyes
stare into my soul

Cats don't even like it
why is it even there?

Library Office Center

Need to scan some paperwork
I put it in the tray
push the button

It's not working
thwarted by a scanner

Wait no...turn the papers around
delete the blank file, try again
what, now the are upside down

Fantasize about throwing
scanner out the window

Flip paper 180 degrees
delete file, try again

Now I have scanned documents
wasn't that easy?

Library Office Center (Indulging in fantasies)

Need to scan some paperwork
I put it in the tray
push the button

It's not working
thwarted by a scanner

Wait no...turn the papers around
delete blank file, try again
What, now they are upside down

I rip the cord from the wall
pick up the scanner
walk three steps and
throw it out the window

The glass shatters
there is a satisfying crunch
as the scanner hits the ground
surrounded by tiny pieces
of broken glass

Returning back to reality
from this amusing fantasy
flip the paper 180 degrees
delete file, try again

Now I have scanned documents
Wasn't that easy?

Library Office Center (How I slayed the monster)

You just won't work
I have tried so many times
I know I have had enough
the anger is building
but I will not be thwarted
by a scanner

I try one more time
the image is upside down
you smile at me
like you know you have won
Oh hell no

I rip your cord from the wall
pick you up
walk three steps and
throw you out the window

The glass shatters
you make a satisfying crunch
as you hit the ground
three stories below
surrounded by tiny pieces
of broken glass

I give a triumphant smile
that turns to panic
as I see the security officers
with their batons
out and ready

I run down the hallway
straight to the stairs
no time to wait
for the elevator

on this trip

I race down three flights
security hot on my trail
quickly out the front door
fresh air gives me hope of escape
I give you two big middle fingers
as I pass you on the ground

Some may think this is stupid
but I think it is worth it
to see that smug smile
wiped clean

Release

Simple white bottle
rounded curves on the sides

strange cap looks like a fez
nozzle hidden inside

I breathe you in
I can't define my need
I lay back as you fill me

I taste you in the back of my mouth
the subtle taste of grapefruit
sparks in my senses

drowning in mounting pressure
but now I am free
as you grant me sweet release

Tim Johnston

Happiness

The happiest day in my life,
will be when anger and hate
release their hold.
When love and compassion
begin to break through
thick, stubborn walls.
When regret and memories
fade into another room
locking the door
not succumbing to their knocking
their screams
to be released.
When the Sun calls to me.
Its rays drying the tears,
wrapped in its arms,
smothering the darkness within.

The Sun

Rising in the East
bright yellow ball.
Rays touching down
warming the grass,
giving hope.
How I miss you
when you are gone.
The warmth of your touch
always fulfilling.
Yes, I miss you
but know that others
need your light
your happiness
to brighten their day.
And when I wake
we will be together again.

3 A.M.

The alarm kicks in the door.
Screams at me.

"Time to get up asshole,
the dreams are done.
They're all bullshit anyways.

Stop bitching and moaning.
You chose this life,
now you answer to me.

Pour yourself a coffee,
go to your shitty job,
collect your pennies.

You're chained to me.
Don't worry though,
you can always break free.

Just open the drawer,
wrap your fingers around the cold
smooth metal,
raise your hand,
open your mouth,
AND PULL!"

9 to 5

The 9 to 5
the image of success,
a fucking nightmare,
a perverted fairytale.

Assholes wrapped in wool,
mindlessly conforming
to a running dialogue
of bullshit and deceit.

A sirens song,
a lyrical lie,
that carries them into the darkness
of their master's desires.

He feasts upon their dreams,
then shits them out
into a golden bowl
of privilege.

The 9 to 5
a faceless life
controlled by a parasite
in an Armani suit.

Thomas Kropp

Tahnee Black Crow(The Dark Witch of Edonia)

This is my world
Death to the Outsiders
And their treacherous allies
With my supernatural power
My sisters will spill their blood
They will take scalps
And I will eat the heart of my enemy
I am the Black Crow
All will fear me

Natayah Sunflower

Adopted from a dead tribe
Born different from others
My husband left me for another
Being a supernatural
I am childless
The Black Crow lay waste to my family
I seek revenge
I will scalp my enemy
I will eat Tahnee's heart
I am the Last Sunflower
The Guardian Ranger is born

The Dark Stairs

The dark stairs
Come up here
I welcome you into my embrace
Warm and inviting
Stay up here
Wake up scared
I can't get out
Here I suffocate
Dark in the night
I beg for air
And pray for morning light

Write about the last place a saw assignment

The Head Honcho

I stand here
Atop of my mountain
High and mighty
My arms folded across my chest
I stare down at you
Demanding eyes
Work harder
Work faster
I enslave you

Books (External)

Words on a page
The feel of the paper
I flip the pages
To find out what happens next
In the next great adventure
What worlds I travel to
To what people I become
What will I discover?

Books (Internal)

You are an artist of words
I feel your paper
Soft and smooth to the touch
As I caress your pages
My eyes dilate with excitement
To be in a world with you
As soul mates
And discover each other

Hannah Fletcher

The happiest day in my life

The happiest day in my life
Will be the day I finally escape.

When the darkest clouds stop following me
Once the shackles grant liberty.
After the black dogs lose their way
Instead of following me.

Every day I see colours
But they're all muted and dazed.
The worst is the glaring grey
Disturbing my everyday gaze.

I wait for the day when the outside doesn't scare
me
A moment when the inside doesn't make me afraid.
I wait for the day my thoughts are collected
Instead of scattered across the floor.

On that day I will run with the rainbows
Find the pot of dreams beneath.
I'll finally feel the sunshine on my skin
Be able to embrace the rain storms underneath.

The happiest day in my life
Will be the day I am finally free.

As I sit...

As I sit here looking at your photograph, and
knowingly caress the black frame
I remember that time never did catch your face
Tell me grandfather where did the wings take you when
you flew away?

The countryside you are walking in seems so calm as
you perch on the fence
Shining sunbeams lean into the camera lens
But the watch you're wearing seems unhappy. Wanting to
tick just one more second.

The diary in your pockets looks worn.
Its pages curling up at the sides and the spine is torn.
I wonder what is written inside it. Is it love or worry
born?
I'll always treasure the greatest gift you gave to me
A bible with details of our family's ancestry dating
back to 1843.

Sometimes looking at your photograph requires a
whisper of whiskey
As sometimes it's hard to accept the things that are
missing
Like the days when we would make things out of trees
Or the walks we would take through dead brown leaves.

And if there is one thing I have left to say.
It's that for thoughts of you to never go away.
After all, you were the one who helped shape me
You're the reason I am wise through my years at all.

Garrett Carroll

The Hillside of the Mountain

I remember the first day I had ever
truly walked outside,
I was young. Six years old.

Of course, I had walked outside before
in some of the days and years prior.

But this time I escaped through
the window of the room
in the back of a bar I lived in.

No, I wasn't in poverty.
It wasn't the room where the liquor
was made in one of those beer silos,
I wasn't a scavenger scrounging
the sticky floors for food and drink,
sleeping underneath the stainless steel
food prep stations on ceramic tile floors.

My Mother and I lived on site, but I
was grounded forever, a foreigner
in a country whose language
I couldn't speak at all.

I crouched and crept through the window,
my slender six-year-old body fitting snug
through the inviting glass,
and I was invited to the hillside
of the mountain,

snow covering the whole ground.
If I fell through the snow
and fell through the ground, I might've
been cast away to some other place,
stepping through the clouds beneath my feet,

the whole world shifting upside-down on me;

in the bliss of Switzerland, I'm already there,
in a reality where I do understand German,
where I am not alone in my brown wooden
bedroom box, desk in place of bed and TV,
isolated and slouched by the corner
of the wooden bed frame, away from the world,
Batman Returns playing on the TV.

Away from the bar, on an impromptu adventure,
a mile away I climb into the gondola lift,
me, an invisible six-year-old
naively afraid of no one, God peering
through the tinted glass of the square box,
the wise observant elder I needed,
or perhaps invited through some
benign pilgrimage this side of the world.

Outside, the sky is a bright blue,
with white clouds covering certain portions
and some strangers with me in the gondola
comment and ask where my parent's are
in German, then in broken english.

I told them I ran away, lonely
and directionless, grounded. I reach
the top of the mountain and roll carelessly
down the slope, snow stitching itself
to my jacket and ski pants as the wind
turns my face tomato red, as my hands
freeze numb and wet.

and I sense they'll be down there
below,
ready to heave me back to the bar
and ask why I left, ask me why I ran away,

prod my childish brain; they'll find every
way to tell me I have
an overly rambunctious mind,
making the clouds flip back over,
closing the door at the concrete edge of other
futures,
ones where life feels special and sacred,
a covenant cracked in hypothermic birth.

I have no skis to fly down the mountain,
just the brunt of my legs and snow boots
to walk and trip over through the rest
of the sloping hillside. I slide walk sideways
down
the mountain slowly and apprehensively.

They await my arrival at the bottom of the slope.
My Mother
and her mustached, mulleted boyfriend standing
right there like imposing statues, watching me
return
to their humorless eyes and lips.

I am returning home, or at least
where I'm told home is, ready to be invited
to the dreams I'll have in scattered isolation.

But for a brief hour, the clouds
at my feet had flipped upside-down,
and I, and I alone and lonely,
felt the comfort of walking free
for the first time with just myself
and God, outside, next to me.

O. Marie

I was 31

Backwards 13

The most unlucky number right?

Except 31 was by far more of a nightmare than 13 could ever be

I was 31 when I was shown what real evil looks like

What I thought was playful flirting from a much younger man turned into making me feel like a used trash receptacle

A man I didn't pay that much attention to

A man I had no interest in

Real evil is wrapped in flattering words and winks

Real evil catches you unawares and literally takes you from behind

Real evil leaves you bleeding and covered in dry semen

Real evil leaves you shaking and questioning everything you ever thought you knew about anything

Real evil is what I've tried to forget for the past eight years

Real evil is living about an hour from my home

Damn him

63

                            smile

Hands groping
Mouth wandering over every inch of me
The taste of our sex on your lips as you smash your
mouth a bit too roughly against mine
Awkward
The kiss was not meant to be so hard
Your eyes gave that away
I think it's adorable
He touch as if he had been thirsting for my body
for a decade and just now getting his first drink
My fingers digging into his broad muscular back
So strong
Not from some gym but from hard manual labor
Able to maneuver me so effortlessly
Lost in the sensations
Fevered from his touch
I have never felt hands that touch so firmly yet so
gently, like a butterfly landing
The slightest of feelings
Goosebumps
So strange
I was groomed to pleasure from the age of fourteen
Detaching the emotional from the physical my only
hope if I wanted to remain functional when I was
out amongst society
I've known so much physical pleasure in my life
So many partners
So many hands and so many mouths
But never have I felt hands like this
Calloused and scarred
Large and fumbling
Careful, so very careful
Why is he doing this?
Is this a sick game?
He knows I want him

I need him
Only him in this moment
He can feel how badly I need release
Why is he acting as if I may break at any moment,
shatter into a million pieces, and just blow away?
He knows enough about me to know he won't hurt me
right?
I've kept it no secret from him
This is not a time for gentleness
I pant in urgency
His breath hitched and eyes that were already
dark turn black
There it is
That's the look I know
Predator
He flips me over
Hands squeeze and separate my thighs and ass
I raise up to my knees
Back arched farther than comfort would allow
He wastes no time and plunges inside me
He thrust long and slow at first
He vocalizes his pleasure as vehemently as I do
It's building
Very fast
His noises only adding to my pleasure
He fucks me harder
I bury my face into the cushions of his couch
I cum
Hard
He feels me tighten and release
He groans and cums hard inside me
Feeling him pulse just making me want more and
more
Don't stop
Oh please don't stop
He punishes himself as he keeps thrusting his
sensitive cock in me

I cum again
He follows
He then lays beside me
Still seemingly needing to touch me
I'm beyond confused at this point
Maybe he recuperates fast
He is ready for another round
Cock still firm against my thigh
Gentle touches to my face
My neck
My collarbone
Down
He cups my already overly stimulated breast
His hands feel like fire on my skin
So careful and so hot
Like being pet on by a flame without being burnt
Why is he being so gentle?
I have never known a touch like this
He leans over and places the softest kiss to my
lips
He climbs on top of me
Places his hard cock inside
Slowly and carefully
His eyes are not so dark now
Strange
I have never had a more intense orgasm
This new feeling was the sexiest thing I had ever
experienced
Emotional melded with the physical
Carefulness and consideration came into play
Tenderness and appreciation once a foreign
concept when sex was involved
I'm a whore for his gentle touch now
I still enjoy the emotionless and mindless sex
Sex that I can lose myself to
But I'm a whore for his passionate sex
I prefer it gently now

I sit, I smile
Hands placed delicately on my lap
A picture of feminine obedience

I sit, I smile
Not a soul aware of the scars I possess
Nobody would know,
Nobody could know

I sit, I smile
My escape playing consistently through my mind
Reaching for peace everyday but always being just
out of touch

I sit, I smile
Cold metal felt against my thigh
A weirdly erotic feeling
Blade hidden from wandering eyes
I could be free right now if I chose
Yet I still sit, and I still smile

Matt Wall

Happiest day in my life

8 cm
Just 2 short
They sent us home
Again
We had to wait
Until 10cm
How the fuck
Am I supposed to
Measure that?

Playing risk
Listening to willie Nelson
It seemed to be
Happening again
This time
It was time

They took us to
The top floor
They said
The baby is coming
But told me
I had to rush
To admin
And check in
It was on the other side
Of the hospital
First floor
I ran faster than ever
Dripping sweat
Out of breath
I wasn't gonna miss this
I wasn't gonna miss
The birth of my child

I screamed at someone
And ran back
Could barely breathe
"It's crowning!" A nurse yelled
She had her up the canal
Holding the baby in place
The doctor wasn't there
And wasn't gonna make it
I apparently turned white
When I saw that hairy head
Come out of that hairy snatch

Another doctor comes in
Does the thing
The woman is squeezing
My hand
It may have been broken
I didn't know then
And don't remember now
The baby came out
The baby was early
So nurses were rushing
To take it down to ICU

I walked behind them
Watched them check
I counted fingers and toes
Looked back at the woman
In time to watch the
Placenta
Fall into a mop
Bucket

They quickly let us hold
The baby
The baby that I had been
Trying to make sure

Would make it into this world
Alive
Someone snapped a pic
Of that first time
I held my child
For that I am glad
Those 7 months
We're the most stressful
Of my life
The kid that every doctor said
Would t make it
Made it

I spent many hours
With my child
In that icu
Placing my pinky
In her tiny hand
Looking into her strange eyes
In shock that she was finally here
And ok

Unchained melody played
I sang it to her
She smiled
I know she probably didn't mean to
But I like to think she did

Before he fakes his own death

Did he kill his mother?
I don't know
He seemed shocked
When I told him she was dead

new ashtray

you're so clean
see-through
I'm just gonna wreck you
ruin your good looks
I know that's your plight
you were created
for me to dirty
it's sad
I feel sorry
for your purpose
but
I won't take that away from you

The man in the window

I paid the cashier
I saw you out the window
Watching me count my money
I put it back in my pocket
And waited until you left
Because I knew you would ask
And I knew I would give it
But this is all I have
I don't know when I'm getting more
Please don't make feel bad
This is all I have

reincarnation

i wonder where
words in poems go
when they die?

right now this poem
is alive
because i'm writing it
but as soon as i finish it
it will be dead
dead to me

i know that poems
have an afterlife
they must
or else you wouldn't
be reading this

what is dead to me
is alive to you
right now
as these words
play across the page
for your eyes

but
do the words of poems
get reincarnated?

if the poems are good
do the words get used
by a greater poet
in an award winning book?
does the greater poet
acknowledge the words
previous life?

do those words
reach an even greater poet
before nirvana?

if the poems are bad
do the words keep dropping
down the ladder
of shittier and shittier
poets
until
they become
an unfinished poem
in a notebook
thrown into a drawer
not to be looked at again
for 40 years
and when they are found
the former poet
says something like
"i remember
when i used to
toy around
with that shit"
before throwing it
into a box
or worse
the trash can

what happens to those words?
where do they go then?
can they come back up the ladder?
can you make beauty
out of shit words
in shit lines
from a shit poem
by a shit poet?

i guess it can happen
i hear poets are the most
notorious thieves
among all of literature

let's see where this ends up...

the talk of reincarnation
happened today
the thought of it
makes me nauseous
who the fuck
would want to go through
all of this shit
all over again?

who would want
another chance
at the struggle
of life?

my whole life
people have told me
that i am or have
an old soul
that i have lived
many many many
lives

this may be why
i have absolutely
no desire
to ever do this shit
again

but that could all be
bullshit

where do we go after?
if it isn't here again?
some of you will be quick
to point out the nursery

rhymes
from the good book
been there
done that
not interested

if that is the case then
what is the alternative?
where do we go?
what do we do?
or better yet
do we do
as this poem should do
and
just
fucking
STOP?

the junky

black coffee
you rule my life
you're my pimp
and i hate you for it

cigarettes
you make me sick
you are my dealer
and i hope to kill you
before you kill me

sex
you run my mind
you are my whore
and i wish you dead

booze
you numb the pain
you are my doctor
but your cost is too high

writing
i can't function without you
you are my master
and i wish i could rebel

me
we are nothing
we are twins
we hate each other and
slowly inch closer
to the end

                      The desk lamps revenge

In the late afternoon
at my desk to write
Flipped the switch
On my desk lamp
And out shone
From the bulb
Complete and utter
Darkness
Horribly opaque
No light in it at all
The black beam
Sounded
As if it were crushing
The things beneath it
I ran my fingers through it
Feeling great pain
I pulled my hand back I grabbed the lamp
And swung it's beam
Around the room
Creaking breaking smashing shattering sounds
breaking silence
The wine gnats and flys
Flew away in a fury
hurriedly
My dirty cum crusted clothes
on the floor
Inched like caterpillars
Towards the safety of the setting sun
My paintings taped to the walls
Pulled away from their adhesive
And rolled tight from the destruction
Everything was failing
Everything was falling apart
I finally shined its full blackness
Onto myself

And soon
I was compacted
Crunched Into the vacuum
The absence of light
And became nothing more
Than an mere idea
A faint memory
Of something that once was
Possibly
At some point
Somewhere
With some purpose
Unfulfilled